The Ruins of the Soul

I0441486

Hamed Vahidi

DENVER, COLORADO

Outskirts Press, Inc.
http://www.outskirtspress.com

ISBN: 978-1-4327-8636-6

Library of Congress Control Number: 2012901109

Outskirts Press and the "OP" logo are trademarks belonging to Outskirts Press, Inc.

PRINTED IN THE UNITED STATES OF AMERICA

To
Seekers of Truth
Prisoners of Fate

Contents

Introduction

The process by which words, images, and sudden flashes of insight enter the mental landscape of a writer and the way he shapes his thoughts and words into poetry, is to some extent inexplicable. I believe this introduction should satisfy the curiosity of readers who demand a detailed and complete explanation.

This book is divided into two parts: lyric poems and Rubaiyat (Rubaiyat is the plural word for Ruba'i or four-line stanza). Lyric poems deal with the inseparable subjects of love and separation. They are not written for a specific person, but rather represent a distinct mood and feeling. I dedicate the poems to all those who find solace in them, especially the people of the Third World countries whose lives are at the mercy of political and economic upheavals.

The first six Ruba'i can be grouped into the category of miscellaneous. The rest deal with the perennial problem of free will. Do humans have free will, or they are simply puppet-like creatures subject to the external and internal forces that govern their lives? The Rubaiyat on free will start from and expand on the notion that humans are endowed with a soul that has the ability to perform acts of free will.

To make it more interesting, I have presented the free will debate in the form of a dialogue between two individuals of sharply different beliefs: Wil and Nil. Wil is a religious person who believes in the soul and the notion of free will. Nil is an agnostic intellectual who denies not only the two concepts of free will and soul, but also the existence of "self."

Free will is a complex subject, and I am just touching the surface by trying to introduce the readers to the basic problems that arise when we claim we have performed an "act of free will." It should also be noted that the two poems "Grave" and "Beloved" were first published in an Internet magazine and they appear here in slightly different versions from the originals.

Lyric Poems

Love and Reason

The careless motion of the rambling wind,
Or the tale of lovers, restless like the wind.

Wind blows with no mind or desire;
Love burns your body like a corpse on a pyre.

The fire molds you into a new creature;
You abandon reason and dance with nature.

The Chosen One

I hear the angels coming as they flap their wings;
The face of the moon pales and the owl sings.

They see a child dying on this cold floor,
Their sole purpose to take away his soul.

Let's paint his ashen look with the color of night.
Maybe the divine vultures will miss him tonight.

Let's hide him in the house of the lewd woman;
The angels are forbidden to turn eyes on this woman.

The grief of the mother as her child writhes in pain,
The joy of heaven as it waits for a new mate to claim.

Some scars leave their marks forever on the soul;
What use to be in heaven when hell is your own soul?

Candle

Once I saw an old man staring at a candle flame,
Frozen like a frame, mentioning God's name in vain.

The candle was the body, the flame its golden hair;
The gentle breeze of the night combed it with care.

Suddenly with eyes as lifeless as a cold grave,
He asked what I saw in this shivering wave.

"I see a luminous beauty kindling this dark night";
"I see a burning flame melting my cold heart";

"I see an Indian beauty dance with a thousand gestures";
"I see the face of my beloved in the heat of the flame."

The old man besieged the candle with his two hands,
His eyes filled with tears, his head above his hands.

"The enchanting moves of a seductress dancer?" he said,
No, the futile struggle of the soul to detach from this world.

The soul is the flame, the candle is the frame;
One seeks transcendence, the other goes down the drain.

The soul, uneasy, tormented, seeking a place on high,
The flesh, slave of lust, grazing this lowly ground.

Soon of that melting beauty nothing will remain,
So much suffering to endure, yet no heaven to attain.

Beloved

The battle of God and Evil to advance their goals,
The failure of both in tending to human souls.

One racks the soul, one sears the flesh with desire;
No mortal is immune from this divine satire,

Freeze the blood in my veins and crush my bone,
But don't come near her grave, leave my beloved alone.

Her fate was sealed when she did not bow to praise God;
She was found dead in a dark dungeon beaten by a rod.

Let me whisper into her ears, let me lie in her nest;
I remember when her body was the castle and I was the guest.

Now the silence weighs upon my back;
The trees share my grief and the air is black.

She looked for the angels and the friendship of the wind;
I grieved at her departure and entrusted her to the wind.

The trembling lips of the grieving lover shake the world;
They repel the angels and bring the wrath of the Lord.

Don't be disturbed by the tears I shed at her grave;
Once she was the master and I was her slave.

Rest in peace my beloved, for you have your own grave;
Countless others are buried together in one grave.

Nature

I am the God, I am the Evil,
I am the mender of lives, I am the render of ties.

I form each creature in the mold of my own nature,
I make every human feel like a special creature.

I bewitch you with the flickering of so many stars;
The beauty of my meadows is the junction of lonely hearts.

But don't be fooled by the allure of so much beauty;
Take a deep look and see what lies beneath.

The book of life is written with the blood of every creature;
I am the author of life and breath, yet my signature is death.

I dance to the beats of my own drum with no goal in mind;
I hide my errors to make things look superbly designed.

My only desire is to get the glimpse of a world beyond mine.
Don't lose hope, rays from that world may someday shine.

Rest Assured

Rest assured you rich of the world,
The poor pray, and great is the Lord.

The God of the rich works in mysterious ways;
The hand of time plays your favorite games.

Don't cry, mother. Your breast has few drops of milk;
Your dress is torn, but your heavenly robe is made of silk.

Your crooked frame, the weeping willow of this land,
The vast shadow, the scene of love affairs so grand.

The rules of the game are unjust and the tactics unfair;
The system allows a chosen few to get the best share.

The butler serves the masters and they let him stay;
The rest are pigeons with heads stuck in clay.

The life of the peasant, a symphony of death and sorrow,
Misery his concubine, everyday he prays for a better tomorrow.

The soul is made of bricks, each one an unfulfilled desire.
Envy the sage who lives in poverty and has no desire.

The Story of Night

The face of the night was once white,
Glorious, glittering, and bright.

The angels looked pale in her presence,
Her beauty boundless and her scope immense.

Plunged in rage, the jealous gods conspired;
They unleashed fire on the jewel they once admired.

She cried in agony, but no one dared to fight the fire;
The smoke rose in the air, no rain to put out the fire.

The night burned and lost her ancient glory;
She became dark and cold, no hope for a future glory.

Today the night is dead, but fire burns with the same might;
The fool praises fire and is appalled by the dark face of the night.

The Heart of the Prophet

Your face is gloomy and your mood somber,
Your voice is weak; once it was the sound of thunder.

"My heart is broken, pounded by unseen hands";
"Soon it shatters and the pieces fall on new lands."

Don't grieve, you have the heart of the prophet;
The savage and the wise want a piece of the prophet.

Your heart is pure and clear, like a stainless mirror;
When it bursts into pieces, each piece is the entire mirror.

The eyes are the gates of the human soul;
When the mirror is broken, thousands see their souls.

The Many Faces of Love

Love is not weak.
The name raises the flames of desire;
A touch sets your entire being on fire.
A picture burns the heart of the mournful mother;
A drop quenches the thirst of the wounded lover.

Love binds.
Wandering lovers in search of their lost loves
Join to become the smooth motion of a single stream.
Upon the naked desert you find their tracks.
Don't cry, they became one before they vaporized.

Love is not fair.
Children lie in their nests with open mouths;
Thousands roam the earth for a loaf of bread.
Few are blessed with the grace of the Beloved;
The others get molten lead in their mouths.

Love is not love,
Unruly and thoughtless, like the waves of the ocean.
Sometimes the ocean roars; sometimes there is no motion.
The lover is doomed, enduring the wrath of a mindless sea,
Pounded by waves, no hope for liberation.

Don't Hide from Me

These are the days of dark clouds and deluge.
Mother holds the skull of her son,
Her withering body bearing a burden so huge.

For a soul in distress, few remedies will suffice -
The hand of God healing the root,
Or an earthly love that extends to Paradise.

Don't hide from me; the sorrows of the world are enough.
Come to me and brighten my day;
Seek another mate, but let me be your eyes' inmate.

Why do you sail in this uproarious sea?
Why do you stand in the rain?
Why do you walk in this dangerous terrain?

Let me be your guide; I'll take you to a safe land.
The sun is hidden, but I have a candle in my hand.
You and I and the candle. The rest of the world is a barren land.

House of Vengeance

See how the new inmate lives in agony,
Confined to a dungeon lit by candles,
Motionless and cold, facing a mirror,
Legs in fetters, neck in chain, heart in pain,

Don't grieve for this creature.
He separated children from their mothers;
Countless men were suffocated under his boot;
Our youth were sent to gallows as he stood tall in his suit.

In punishment, the gods found him the perfect mate.
The friction of the gazes sparked a love so great,
His face radiant, he was now a new breed.
Soon all his prisoners were freed.

Suddenly, the wolves were summoned to kill his lover.
The manner was so gruesome he could not breathe.
Her breasts were torn; the scene made his eyes bleed.
His beloved was gone; he could not go on,

The House of Vengeance is the final punishment;
Every day, he sees his beloved's face in the mirror.
He moans and groans until the image fades away;
He is now silent, waiting for the next day.

Veil

Don't unveil.
The rest of you bedims your august eyes;
Your grace betrays the honesty of your cries.

You groan in agony; the world has done you wrong,
Your suffrage exceeds the confines of sanity.
Your pain brings every human to the verge of insanity.

Let your eyes be the asylum for my tormented soul;
Let them be nourishment to this indignant soul;
Let them shine in darkness and brighten my soul.

Countless years I wandered in search of joy and flesh;
Roads I traveled seeking a mate noble and fresh.
Fruitless were my efforts and weakened was my flesh.

Now that I find you, my journey ends in your eyes.
The wind flirts with your veil and my soul flies;
The darkness that cloaks your body, my eternal house.

The Comfort of the Soul

When the head is worthless and the mind untidy,
When you wait for years for the help of the almighty,

When the voice of the wind is a sigh in despair,
When the world is your opponent and the game unfair,

When the tidings of your beloved lead you to her grave,
When the sun leaves children cold in the grave,

When the moon fears the night and the sun is ashamed of the day,
When the wings of the vultures dim the light of the day,

Sail into the vast ocean of your soul.
Don't fear; you are the only one in control.

Secret of the Wind

Break the silence and reveal your secret, O Wind;
You are that defiant rebel who can never be pinned.

You ramble through the meadows with such ease;
Your freedom is a castle that can never be seized.

You flirt with the desert and touch her naked breast;
You engulf her body and make love to her with zest.

You touch the skin of lovers and they go insane;
Who is not moved by your majesty is truly insane,

Crush my bones and dump my body in a pit,
Then lift me with your strength and revive my spirit.

Empty my veins and infuse them with your breath.
Why shed blood for those who won't hold a breath?

Whirlpool

Head envies the heart's serenity;
Heart is appalled by the head's rigidity;

Soul is repelled by the longings of the flesh;
Evil mocks the soul and elevates the flesh.

I am the leaf thrown into this whirlpool.
Why does my fate have to be so cruel?

Blind Alley

I leave the caravan behind; the wind brings me back.
I run to my destiny; a voice tells me to come back.

I stay with the caravan and think,
"Are they humans or a flock of sheep?"

Learned or pious, each tells a different story;
They march forward and tell me not to worry.

The learned say, "The world has no purpose or goal;"
"We have now matured; we don't need the notion of soul."

"Rejoice! Rejoice! We have killed God;"
"Let's move on and bury the memory of that fraud."

"Whoever longs for heavenly virgins and immortality,"
"He is a fool, there is a flaw in his mentality."

"Let's build a new world and forget the hereafter;"
"Let's be our own Gods and start a new chapter."

"Forget religion and rely on your own mind;"
"For once prove you belong to a superior kind."

The pious present their own brand of rhetoric,
A world of angels and a God who cares for the sick.

"Eternal life," they say, "this is what makes humans complete;"
"Man is restless till the day he and his God meet."

"Man without a soul is a piece of flesh;"
"The breath of God makes the dead start afresh."

"Your sufferings will be recorded in the book of the divine;"
"When you reach heaven, you will achieve a station sublime."

My beloved and I have suffered wounds and calamities;

We have endured the wrath of God and worldly enemies.

Tender is her kiss and so green is our valley,
Sometimes I forget that the world is a blind alley.

When the ocean is unruly and the suffering immense,
The faith of my forefathers outweighs logic and sense.

Insane

I abandoned the world;
The demons do not leave me.
I gave up the sword;
The streams of blood incite me.

I drank wine with Satan;
The wrath of God scares me.
I sought shelter in heaven;
The evils of this world haunt me.

I turned to my beloved;
Found her in the corner of a dark alley,
Her eyes closed, her face loaded with pain.
I damned the two worlds and went insane.

Grave

Come see the grave where the rest of me is confined;
She was the spool on which the threads of my heart would wind.

The dimple of her cheek was the chalice for lovers of wine;
Now it's the place where loathsome creatures dine.

The sight of her face awakened my desire;
Now it's a reminder of everything sad and dire.

The pupil of her eye was the dark road I took with no fear;
Dare to enter now, it is the eternal house of pain and tears.

Gaze upon this damned place where humans flock like crows;
They mistake the sigh of the wind for the voice of their fellows.

See how every man squats near a grave growing old beyond his years;
See how every woman enriches the soil with the liquid of her tears.

Beware of the day when memories float away on the sea of time;
No one has the strength to resist a force this sublime.

So let me lie in the grave and hold her hands forever;
The time will pass and our bodies will fade together.

What Is Love?

The loss of the beloved wreaks havoc in your world.
The citadel of your hopes crumbles;
The tower of your desires tumbles;
Your soul darkens and grief becomes your new Lord.

The depth of her gaze and the power of her words
Shielded you from the calamities of the two worlds.
Now the angel is gone and the wounds are open,
But don't grieve, the secret of love will now be open.

A new face brings excitement and mystery;
The sweet taste of the lips did indeed change history.
The story of the slain lovers brings tears into eyes;
One wonders where the secret of such love lies.

Love is not there,
Just a typhoon in the domain of your soul.
The beloved is not there,
Just a change in the seasons of your soul.

When the winter casts her shadow, the lovers depart;
They seek a new face and the beats of a new heart.
Be faithful to your lover and keep all seasons spring;
When she is gone, a new one may spring.

Perplexed

I hear the roar of the lion;
The jungle is silent.
I see the face of the angels;
My soul is in torment.

I crave the freedom of doves;
My knees are broken.
I long for heavenly mansions;
My fortune is taken.

I look into the well;
I see the face of a fool.
I pray to God;
He drags me under his rule.

I walk for days in the heat of the sun;
I don't see a soul in this barren land.
I bury myself deep in the ground;
Thousands stretch their arms to lend me a hand.

If I die, I lose the battle;
If I live, I'll be a sheep in the cattle.
Man is a strange creature,
Never at ease with his own nature.

My Mangled Heart

Sweet companion, my mangled heart,
You pumped blood into my veins.
You followed me into the lion's den
When I fluttered like a wounded hen.

You were my bed-fellow
In the dark comers of prison,
Ribs broken, disease-stricken,
Falsely accused of treason.

Restless in the time of love,
Ferocious when I craved for lust,
You followed me in every adventure,
Gentle and firm; this is your true nature.

When the force of desire cannot conceal the pain,
When shame is so great it paralyzes the brain,
When the body is like a lifeless terrain,
It is your divine melody that keeps me sane.

Joy and Pain

Come and spill my blood, but first,
Grant me a joy that quenches my thirst.

Let the angels kiss me, let my soul refresh;
It eases the pain of my torn flesh.

Don't let countless men live in despair;
Give a little joy before you give pain. Be fair.

Time Travel

Once I had a vision I could travel into the past.
The cosmos was laid on the sea of eternity,
Glittering, limitless, and vast.

I saw dark tunnels thinner than hair,
Doorways to the past.
What if I could rekindle a long-dead affair?

Soon I found myself in another time and place;
Sitting next to me was my beloved.
How could I describe the splendor of her grace?

I felt the heat of her body and begged for an embrace,
But she gave me a cold shoulder;
For a moment I thought I was in the wrong place.

Suddenly she turned to me and said in a soft voice,
"Every day I see a new imitation of you."
"Don't set your hopes high, you are my last choice!"

"This is the beginning of your journey through time."
"Continue your search and I promise,"
"Someday you'll find a version of me that fits you fine."

Alley of the Friends

I see the smoke rising in the air;
Bodies are naked, souls in despair.
The sky looks closer and gray;
The demons have come to slay.

I hear the sigh of the girls
As their gardens are grubbed for more joy.
I hear the laugh of the gardeners
As they spade up the gardens with more joy.

Children fight over a piece of bread;
People run from the living and the dead.
The walls are stained with blood;
The road is filled with clod.

I see my daughter lying in her nest,
Her body savaged with infinite zest.
She desired to be the maiden of God one day,
A day when she would dress in white and pray.

My wife, the woman who made my heart palpitate,
My faithful companion in the prison of fate,
Once her breasts made me drunk to the verge of insanity;
No man dared to desire her for I would unleash calamity.

The angels had promised us the kingdom of light,
A land where days did not turn into night.
We lighted the caves and drank from the springs;
The love we shared was the envy of the kings.

Now she looks pale and milk is frozen in her breast;
A deep sense of sorrow weighs upon her chest.
I feel the cold skin of dagger and the blow of a fist;
I never let go of her till my hand is cut from the wrist.

Alley of the friends, this is where my life ends;
The custom is to torture the soul before it ascends.
Is this the way humans are purified and cleansed?
How much suffering till this madness ends?

Spring

I heard the nightingale commencing the spring;
My heart drenched in joy and my lips began to sing.

I abandoned the world and ran away with the wind.
What if the gods knew how much she and I sinned?

We rolled on the meadows and layers of daisy beds;
She told me of the joys of freedom and the tears she sheds.

The secrets she whispered to me no mortal can hear;
She spoke of the eternal life and the pains so severe.

She summoned the rabbits, gazelles, and the birds;
The joyous feast reminded me of newlyweds.

She combed the surface of the river, causing a gentle motion;
Soon the limpid water would join the big ocean.

The river runs by the forces that control her destiny;
If I have no will, then let the ocean be my final destiny.

Rubaiyat

Miscellaneous

The fate of my forefathers shatters my dream;
The suffering of Man is God's favorite theme.
I seek shelter in the verdant meadow of her eyes,
The taste of her tears sweeter than a heavenly stream.

Cry, mother, while the ocean is calm;
Feed your children and gather more crumbs.
The waves are restless again; the gods are coming.
Hide! Hide! I hear the beat of the drums.

Father slays his son with a swing of his sword;
Mother kills her child in the name of the Lord.
I know what lies behind the ocean of tears -
A robotic flesh, forever the slave of the Word.

The gods play with the heads of our sons.
Fate throws them in the path of pythons.
Grant us mercy, O angels of the divine;
Such blisters have burned the earth for eons.

The wisdom of the gods has deeper meaning;
The absurdity of life has deeper meaning.
Show me a philosopher who is not perplexed:
When you reach Heaven, life has no meaning.

When you die and set foot on the other side,
When the Lord of heaven makes you a bride,
You look back at this lowly ground and wonder,
Who was that fool who always moaned and cried?

On Free Will

Nil:

Examine Man in the totality of his being:
If he sees death at the end, why does he go on living?
Fire burns in the flames of its own nature;
Man is more complex, but he is not a free being.

Wil:

I am not a piece of flesh; I have a soul.
I am conscious and in control.
Man is the architect of his own fate;
Only a fool denies the freedom of the soul.

Nil:

What afflicts the body torments the soul;
There are no angels or ultimate goal.
You are the slave of your own desires;
Your destiny is beyond your control.

Wil:

Man is the jewel of God's creation,
He rejects his desires of his own volition.
I am the master of my own passions,
For I can resist the winds of seduction.

The concept of will is easy to define:
I am not under pressure; I am perfectly fine.
I consider the alternatives and then act;
The will is the cause, and the choice is mine.

Nil:

You are conscious of what you yearn for;
You may reach for it or open another door.
But the truth is that you are just an observer,
Driven by the opposing forces on this infinite shore.

You save your children from the uproarious sea;
You comfort them and call this act free.
Whoever does otherwise, you say, is insane,
For this is the way a human should be.

Wait until you hear the call of the Beloved;
It asks for blood and countless bodies to behead.
You sacrifice your children and call this act free;
If asked for more, you offer your own head!

One mother beats her baby until he dies;
The other runs to her child when he cries.
Who acted freely, and who was compelled?
One goes to the gallows; the other is idolized.

Wil:

But what remains of man if he has no will?
Who should be held responsible, and who is ill?
Life will become meaningless and hollow.
The foundation of ethics will be nil.

Nil:

Maybe there is a glimpse of hope after all,
But you need to be learned and rational.
Think deeply and reflect on your actions;
This is what distinguishes you from a mindless doll.

A man of reason will never succumb to persuasion.
He weighs his thoughts before taking action.
He thinks logically and has a keen mind -
Traits that give him the power of rational negation.

Don't think that your wish has come true;
Not even the rational is free; sad but true.
Let's sail together in the ocean of my words,
For this is the best you and I can do!

The rational is like a robot with a human side,
The interplay of genes, brain and the world outside.
The force of reason compels the host to act,
Yet a free agent is always assumed to be the guide.

What if the body is imbued with a soul?
What if one substance is in control?
The absence of will is independent of Time;
It applies to both the flesh and the soul.

Some say the flesh is run by the soul,
That soul is the only agent in control.
But who says the chain should stop here?
What lies behind the soul?

Souls are not free in the next world;
They are the toys of Satan or the Lord.
Some wish to return; some cry and mourn:
The same sorrows exist in the next world.

You were blind and suddenly are aware;
You command at will and begin to compare.
A selection is made and the chapter is closed.
Was it "You" who made you aware?

From the point you start till the end of the game,
Grab a section of Time and analyze each frame.
Go to the deepest level to search for your Self.
All I see is the dance of particles, with no end or aim.

The body labels the soul as the true Self.
Even a free soul refers to his own "Self";
If the Self is real, then where does it lie?
You don't need a Self to be aware of yourself.

I can imagine a robot that recognizes itself,
A machine that learns from its errors and repairs itself.
One day it may gain the power to judge and reason;
If so, does it matter whether it is really aware of itself?

I took refuge in love as a last resort.
It made me a slave; love's promise fell short.
The only free being is a deluded being.
I know what to say when I enter the Divine Court.

Wil:

Your words make life not worth living.
What glory, then, to be a human being?
Who cares if humans are not free?
The gift of soul makes me an immortal being.

I'm neither a zombie nor a secular beast;
I use reason but see no reason to exist.
The promise of heaven gives meaning to my life;
When I die, the angels will invite me to their feast.

Nil:

Cherish my verses and take this advice:
The wrongdoers will someday pay the price.
The judge sees your actions, not your pain.
What will it take to change your path to Paradise?

Wil:

The signature of Evil lies at every foundation,
Randomness and chaos are the tools of creation.
The path to Paradise is through nature,
From emptiness comes a God who is beyond contradiction.

www.ingramcontent.com/pod-product-compliance
Lightning Source LLC
Chambersburg PA
CBHW070842310526
45793CB00011B/505